Cornerstones of Freedom

The Story of

SHERMAN'S MARCH TO THE SEA

By Zachary Kent

Illustrated by Ralph Canaday

 CHILDRENS PRESS®

CHICAGO

Library of Congress Cataloging-in-Publication Data

Kent, Zachary.
   The story of Sherman's march to the sea.

   (Cornerstones of freedom)
   Summary: Describes the devastation incurred by the
Union general's march from Atlanta to Savannah during
the Civil War—an act which hastened the Confederate
surrender by destroying the South's economic resources.
   1.   Sherman's March to the Sea—Juvenile literature.
2.   Sherman, William T. (William Tecumseh), 1820-
1891—Juvenile literature.   [1.   Sherman's March to the
Sea.   2.   Sherman, William T. (William Tecumseh), 1820-
1891.   3.   United States—History—Civil War, 1861-1865]
I.   Canaday, Ralph, ill.   II.   Title.   III.   Series.
E476.69.K46   1987   973.7'378   86-31054
ISBN 0-516-04728-0

Great sheets of roaring flame towered hundreds of feet above the rooftops. Huge clouds of swirling sparks and floating cinders choked the air. No witness would ever forget the night of November 15, 1864, in Atlanta, Georgia. As burning factory floors collapsed, metal machinery crashed down into basements. Weakened brick walls swayed together and tumbled into formless heaps. The booming of exploding armory shells and gunpowder, together with the panic of galloping horses and the wild shouts of excited men, created a nightmarish scene.

After they had occupied Atlanta for six weeks, the blue-clad Union troops had received orders to destroy everything of value to the Confederate enemy. So that night, eager enlisted men torched the city's railroad depot, engine roundhouse, foundries, machine shops, and mills. Soon fires sprang up in the city's hotels, theaters, and dry-goods stores. The Atlanta jail and slave market buildings were also quickly engulfed by flames.

On street corners, gleeful soldiers danced and sang. Some broke windows and looted stores. Others set fire to private homes just to watch the flames. Before long the night glowed so brightly that, in a Yankee camp a mile and a half away, Minnesota private Axel Reed exclaimed, "We could see to read newspapers at midnight . . . from the light of burning buildings."

One lean, grim Union officer, with reddish hair and a short, rough beard, walked through the streets surveying the damage around him. On the shoulders of his plain, smoke-stained uniform were the twin stars that marked him as a major general. William Tecumseh Sherman understood the horrors of war perhaps better than any soldier in the North or South. Now, in a bold, sweeping move, he intended to show the Southern people those horrors. Already, columns of Union troops waited on the Georgia roads stretching to the southeast. By leading this hardened army on a three-hundred-mile march of destruction to Savannah and the sea, Sherman promised, "I can . . . make Georgia howl!"

Since 1861 the United States had been gripped in a bloody civil war. A long, raging argument over slavery had torn the country in two. In the North, where factories abounded, thousands of European immigrants were willing to work cheaply. Northerners had no use for slavery, and many people considered it to be cruel and immoral. The South, however, greatly depended upon slavery for the success of its farming economy.

The problem reached its crisis when Abraham Lincoln was elected sixteenth president of the United States in November 1860. Many Southerners feared that Lincoln, a Northerner from Illinois, would abolish slavery. The Southern states insisted that the federal government had no right to force laws upon the states.

One by one, Southern states quit the Union—first South Carolina, Florida, Georgia, Alabama, Mississippi, Louisiana, and Texas; and later Virginia, North Carolina, Arkansas, and Tennessee. Together these seceded states formed the Confederate States of America, with Jefferson Davis as its president. In April 1861 the American Civil War began when Confederate cannon fired on Fort Sumter in Charleston harbor, forcing federal troops to withdraw.

In Washington, President Lincoln quickly called for volunteers to put down the rebellion. Anxiously he searched for experienced military officers to lead these troops into battle. One such soldier was a forty-one-year-old West Point graduate named William T. Sherman. Though born in Ohio, Sherman had spent many years living in the South. With the start of the war, however, he firmly resolved, "I will do no act, breathe no word, think no thought hostile to the government of the United States."

While serving under General Ulysses S. Grant during the battles of Shiloh, Vicksburg, and Chattanooga, Sherman had grown into an excellent officer.

Though bullets grazed him and horses were shot from under him, Sherman remained in the thick of every fight, calmly shouting orders. In 1864, when General Grant traveled to Virginia to fight against Confederate general Robert E. Lee, he left Sherman in command of the Union's western army.

August of 1864 found Sherman and his veteran troops pressing toward the industrial city of Atlanta, Georgia. On August 9 Sherman wrote to his wife, "I have cannonaded Atlanta pretty heavily today, and our lines are extended full ten miles, but still the enemy is beyond." To the chief of staff, General Henry Halleck, he telegraphed, "We keep hammering away all the time, and there is no peace, inside or outside of Atlanta." Only after a bloody five-week siege did the stubborn rebel army finally retreat.

"Atlanta is ours, and fairly won," Sherman excitedly wired North. As Yankee troops cheered in the Atlanta streets and threw their hats into the air, their general was already planning his next move. In enemy territory, Sherman realized, "the entire South, man, woman, and child, is against us." He later insisted, "We are not fighting hostile armies, but a hostile people, and must make old and young, rich and poor, feel the hard hand of war."

As Sherman developed his idea of "total warfare,"
he came to believe that if the Southern people "can-
not be made to love us," they "can be made to fear
us, and dread the passage of troops through the
country." To destroy the enemy's will to fight, Sherman suggested a march across Georgia to Savannah,
"smashing things to the sea."

With General Grant's permission, Sherman pre-
pared his army for the march. In the Union camps
around Atlanta soldiers loaded ammunition, coffee,
sugar, and pork onto wagons. Night and day,

officers on horseback galloped back and forth,
delivering messages and yelling instructions. On the
railroad, trains carried the army's sick and injured
troops north to safety. The lean soldiers who
remained were tough and self-assured. Private
Theodore Upson proudly explained: "Such an Army
as we have I doubt if ever was got together before;
all are in the finest condition. We have weeded out
all the sick, feeble ones and all the faint hearted ones
and all the boys are ready for a meal or a fight and
don't seem to care which it is."

As they packed their haversacks and filled their canteens, few of the men seemed afraid. Wrote young John Cutter to his father, "Every man under Sherman has the greatest confidence in him, and make up their minds that where he strikes it is sure death to all rebs within his range." An excited officer scribbled in his diary, "I wouldn't miss going on this expedition for 6 months pay." From private to colonel, each man felt he was about to take part in something special.

On November 12, Yankee regiments began destroying the railroad north of Atlanta. Hundreds of men tore up the metal rails and heated them across great bonfires of cross-ties. When the middles of the rails turned red hot, the soldiers picked them up by both ends and twisted them around telegraph poles and trees. Thus the rails, some of them bent to form the letters *U* and *S*, were rendered completely useless to the enemy.

On November 15, as Atlanta burned, Union troops began filing onto the roads leading southeast. At seven o'clock the next morning Sherman joined one column, riding on his favorite horse, Sam. Behind him, two hundred acres of Atlanta now lay in smoldering ashes. Pausing on a hill, the general saw "the

black smoke rising high in the air and hanging like a pall over the ruined city." Shifting in his saddle, he next observed thousands of "gun-barrels glistening in the sun" and "white-topped wagons stretching away to the south." Crowded beside him on the road, his excited men marched "steadily and rapidly, with a cheery look and swinging pace." A regimental band began playing "John Brown's Body" and the men loudly sang along. "Never before or since," commented Sherman, "have I heard the chorus of 'Glory, glory, hallelujah!' done with more spirit."

Grinning and laughing, the soldiers strode forward on the start of their great adventure. Split into two wings and marching in four columns on widely separated roads, Sherman's army consisted of 62,000 men. Most of them from the midwestern states, each foot soldier carried a musket and bayonet and eighty rounds of ammunition. Whatever else he lugged along—tin cup, mess knife, rolled blanket, poncho, and extra pair of socks, or perhaps a clean shirt—was entirely up to him. But as the soldiers were expected to march fifteen miles a day, experience had taught them to travel as lightly as possible. The cavalrymen and cannoneers who rode in comfort on horseback or seated on horse-drawn caissons often traded jokes and insults as they passed their dusty comrades on the roads.

Having boldly cut off its lines of communication, this Union army seemed to disappear into the heart of Georgia. Earlier Sherman had warned Grant, "I will not attempt to send couriers back, but trust to the Richmond papers to keep you well advised." Of the general's unexpected plunge deep into hostile country, *The British Army & Navy Gazette* declared, "He has done either one of the most brilliant or one of the most foolish things ever performed by a military leader." Few people could guess the general's destination. In Washington, when asked where Sherman was and where he was going, President Lincoln could only smile and say, "I know what hole he went in at."

Without a base of supplies, Sherman depended on the bounty of the Georgia countryside to feed his hungry men. "Georgia has a million inhabitants," reasoned the general. "If they can live, we should not starve." On the march he ordered that every brigade send a daily party of soldiers out to gather "meat of any kind, vegetables, corn-meal, or whatever is needed by the command."

Sherman's enthusiastic foragers soon learned to take everything they wanted from the Georgia farms they passed. Major Sam Merrill of the Seventieth Indiana Regiment watched one band of foragers return to camp at sundown on a wide variety of captured carts and wagons. "At the head of the procession [was] an ancient family carriage, drawn by a goat, a cow with a bell, and a jackass. Tied behind . . . a sheep and a calf, the vehicle loaded down with pumpkins, chickens, cabbages, guinea fowl, carrots, turkeys, onions, squashes, a shoat, sorghum, a looking-glass, an Italian harp, sweetmeats, a peacock, a rocking chair, a gourd, a bass viol, sweet potatoes, a cradle, dried peaches, honey,

a baby carriage, peach brandy and every other imaginable thing a lot of fool soldiers could take in their heads to bring away."

Realizing the fun and profit of foraging, other soldiers soon broke ranks each day to swarm over the countryside. These men, called "bummers," left their mark wherever they went. On her plantation near Covington, Georgia, a young widow named Dolly Sumner Bunge suffered one of the wild visits. "Like demons they rushed in!" she grieved. "My yards are full. To my smoke-house, Dairy, Pantry, Kitchen, and Cellar, like famished wolves they came, breaking locks and whatever is in their way."

In Hillsboro, Georgia, bummers raided Mrs. Louise Cornwell's farm four days in a row. When the last group found nothing remaining in the house to steal, a soldier ordered: "Get out. . . . We're gonna burn it down." With quiet dignity Mrs. Cornwell stood with her women relatives. "If you burn our house," she replied, "you'll burn us too. We will not leave. You've taken everything we owned. Now burn us up if you will, for we will not get out." Ashamed by this Southern woman's show of courage, the looters rode away.

Other Georgians were not so lucky. Major James Austin Connolly of Illinois wrote: "Every stack of fodder we can't carry along is burned; every barn filled with grain is destroyed; in fact everything that can be of use to the Rebels is either carried off by our foragers or set on fire and burned."

At least one group of Georgians welcomed the advance of Sherman's army. Every day black slaves thronged the roadsides and greeted the marching soldiers with roaring cheers. Many of these old men, women, and even children understood that the war was being fought because of slavery. Now as they flocked to the soldiers, they guessed their lifelong dream had come true. Major Connolly remarked,

"Negroes stare at us with open eyes and mouths, but generally before the whole column has passed they pack up their bundles and march along, apparently satisfied they are going . . . toward freedom."

"They thought it was freedom now or never," remembered an Illinois artilleryman, "and would follow whether or no. . . . Some in buggies, costly and glittering; some on horseback, the horses old and blind, and others on foot; all following up in right jolly mood, bound for ease and freedom."

Day after day Sherman's columns swept forward, meeting little resistance from the rebel enemy. When the Union army left Atlanta, stunned Confederate leaders had called for immediate action. Southern general P. T. Beauregard urged Georgians, "Arise for the defense of your native soil!" From Richmond several Georgia congressmen telegraphed: "Let every man fly to arms—Every citizen with his gun . . . can do the work of a soldier."

With most of Georgia's healthy men off fighting in Tennessee and Virginia, the only troops remaining consisted of the state's hastily-gathered local militia. On November 22, 3,700 of these old men and

boys attacked the marching Union line near Griswoldville. Brave but poorly trained, these rebel soldiers charged again and again. They had no way of knowing the Yankees here possessed the deadly new Spencer repeating rifle. One sixteen-year-old Georgian, J. J. Eckles, took refuge in a ravine and counted twenty-seven bullet holes in his rolled blanket. After the rebels retreated at last, Union Captain Wills walked the littered battlefield. "Old grey haired and weakly looking men and little boys, not over 15 years old, lay dead or writhing in pain. I did pity those boys," he said. But the bloody fight at Griswoldville hardly slowed the Federal advance.

Meanwhile, the left wing of Sherman's army reached Milledgeville, which was Georgia's state capital in 1864. Days earlier, Governor Joseph Brown and other state officials had fled the town in panic. Those families that remained scurried about, hiding their valuables. With shovels women buried jewelry, silver, clothing, and even slabs of bacon in their gardens and yards. Clever bummers later found many of these treasures by stabbing into the dirt with their bayonets.

Twenty-one-year-old Anna Maria Green sadly watched as the Union troops entered the town. "We were despondent," she remembered, "our heads bowed and our hearts crushed—the Yankees in

possession of Milledgeville. The Yankee flag waved from the Capitol."

Inside the statehouse, a number of drunken Union officers staged a mock session of the legislature. The rowdy scene attracted thousands of other soldiers, who soon ransacked the building, including the state library. Hundreds of books were thrown from the windows onto the wet ground below. As they piled up, soldiers trampled over them, keeping whatever volumes they wanted. This saddened some of the educated officers. Observed Major Connolly, "I don't object to stealing horses, mules . . . and all such *little things*, but I will not engage in plundering and destroying public libraries."

For two days, regiment after regiment passed through the town. Without pausing, the army continued southward, living off the land and leaving the country burnt behind them. At the end of each day the columns stopped by the roadsides, and soldiers, as happy and relaxed as holiday campers, collected firewood, cooked their suppers, and found straw or soft pine branches for bedding. "The weather was fine, the roads good, and everything seemed to favor us," remarked General Sherman.

The march grew more difficult, however, as the army drew closer to Savannah. The lovely pine groves and sandy soil of central Georgia soon gave way to south Georgia's swampy country with its twisting streams and thick forests. One cavalryman, J. W. Bartmess, later informed his wife. "If you want an Idea of the face of this country just think of the swampiest country you ever seen, and then imagine one a hundred times swampier, and you have it." The moss-hung trees were so dense they blotted out the sun. Another soldier, Ole Kittelson, complained, "It was so dark that we couldn't see our hands but it soon lighted up with cussing and swearing that came out of every soldier's mouth as they tramped through the swamp up to the ears."

There were few rich plantations in this region to raid for food. Now Sherman's foragers often returned to camp with empty wagons. After three days without rations, Private Francis Baker and his fellow soldiers of the Seventy-Eighth Ohio Regiment were told by their colonel: "Well, boys, the only thing I can advise is to draw in your belt one more hole each day." In desperation the hungry soldiers soon learned how to hull the rice that was the major local crop. Captain John Storrs of Connecticut remarked, "Our diet was rice for breakfast, rice for dinner, rice for supper, and then more rice."

As the army neared Savannah, Confederate resistance stiffened. On December 8 several Union soldiers were badly injured by the explosion of a mine on one road. Angrily General Sherman ordered rebel prisoners ahead to clear the path of its other mines. Two days later while riding along a railroad track, Sherman spotted a cannon half a mile ahead. "Scatter," he ordered. "They'll give us a shot." He saw the white puff of smoke and spotted the cannonball rising through the air. Though Sherman moved aside in time, a black man nearby was less fortunate. The cannonball struck the ground and then, bouncing up, carried the poor man's head away.

By December 13, 1864, Sherman's soldiers could smell the salt air of the Atlantic Ocean. Only Fort McAllister, a Confederate stronghold on the Ogeechee River south of Savannah, stood between the Yankees and U.S. Navy ships waiting at the seacoast. Climbing to the roof of a nearby rice mill, Sherman watched as General William Hazen's division assaulted the fort. "We saw Hazen's troops come out of the dark fringe of woods," Sherman later explained, "the lines dressed as on parade, with colors flying, and moving forward with quick, steady pace. Fort McAllister was then all alive, its big guns belching forth dense clouds of smoke." The men charged, and when the smoke cleared fifteen minutes later, cheering blue-clad soldiers stood on the battlements waving a U.S. flag. By the following

day Union supply boats were bringing ashore food, clothing, and even mail from home.

The march from Atlanta to the sea was now complete; it signaled the doom of the Confederacy. In less than a month Sherman's men had sliced the South in two, leaving a path of destruction sixty miles wide and three hundred miles long. Behind them, 317 miles of railroad track had been twisted around trees. The charred ruins of mills, factories, and farms filled the Georgia landscape. The Union army had seized 6,871 mules and horses and 13,294 head of cattle. It had captured or destroyed millions of pounds of grains and other food supplies. Remarked army surgeon J. C. Patton: "I think that they will be able to see our track for a generation to come. We have laid a heavy hand on Georgia."

General Sherman made no apology to Southerners for his ruthlessness. "If the people raise a howl against my barbarity and cruelty," he stated, "I will answer that war is war, and not popularity-seeking." To an officer he later grimly added, "The more awful you can make war, the sooner it will be over . . . war is hell, at the best."

Sherman's march to the sea made him a hero throughout the North and brought his army lasting glory. On December 21 Savannah surrendered after a brief siege, further proving the hopelessness of the Southern cause. To President Lincoln, Sherman sent the message: "I beg to present you as a Christmas-gift the city of Savannah." In January the general put his troops on the road again, marching them into South Carolina. The final victory of the war awaited his relentless, unbeatable soldiers in just a few short months. But as they tramped northward they proudly sang the words of the popular song that already marked their greatest triumph:

Our camp-fires shone bright on the mountains
    That frowned on the river below,
While we stood by our guns, in the morning,
    And eagerly watched for the foe,

When a rider came out from the darkness
    That hung over mountain and tree,
And shouted, "Boys, up! and be ready!
    For Sherman will march to the sea!" ...

Then sang we a song for our Chieftain,
    That echoed o'er river and lea,
And the stars on our banner shone brighter
    When Sherman marched down to the sea!

About the Author

Zachary Kent grew up in the town of Little Falls, New Jersey. He is a graduate of St. Lawrence University and holds a teaching certificate in English. Following college he was employed at a New York City literary agency for two years until he decided to launch a career as a writer. To support himself while writing, he has worked as a taxi driver, a shipping clerk, and a house painter.

Mr. Kent has had a lifelong interest in American history. As a boy the study of the United States presidents was his special hobby. His collection of presidential items includes books, pictures, and games, as well as several autographed letters.

About the Artist

Ralph Canaday has been involved in all aspects of commercial art since graduation from the Art Institute of Chicago in 1959. He is an illustrator, designer, painter, and sculptor whose work has appeared in many national publications, textbooks, and corporate promotional materials. Mr. Canaday lives in Hanover Park, Illinois, with his wife Arlene, who is also in publishing.